RIVERS

A Cherrytree Book

Designed and produced by
A S Publishing

First published 1989
by Cherrytree Press Ltd
a subsidiary of
The Chivers Company Ltd
Windsor Bridge Road
Bath, Avon BA2 3AX

Copyright © Cherrytree Press Ltd 1989

British Library Cataloguing in Publication Data
Elder   F. 91   14.58
Mariner, Tom
   Rivers.
1. Rivers. ~~For children~~
   I. Title II. Atkinson, Mike III. Series
   551.4813

   ISBN 0-7451-5048-9

Printed in Italy by Imago Publishing Ltd

EARTH IN ACTION

RIVERS

By Tom Mariner
Illustrated by Mike Atkinson

CHERRYTREE BOOKS

Water of Life

Water is essential to life. From the beginning of human history, people have looked for sources of clean, fresh water. Rivers have provided that water. The principal civilizations of early times grew up by great rivers, and the greatest cities in the world today developed from riverside settlements.

Rivers provide drinking water not only for people but also for their crops. They provide an easy means of transport for people and their goods. They also provide us today with much hydroelectric power. In the past, through ignorance, people allowed rivers to become polluted but now most countries are making sure that poisonous waste from agriculture and industry is not dumped in them.

From the Mountains to the Sea

Even the greatest rivers start in a small way, as a thin trickle of water from a melting glacier or a tiny spring high in the mountains. As the little stream flows swiftly downhill, other streams – *tributaries* – flow into it. Gathering strength, the young river matures into middle age, slowing its pace and broadening into old age as it flows towards the sea.

As the river flows to the sea, more and more water flows into it. The area of land through which the river and its tributaries flow is called its *basin*. The largest river basin in the world is that of the Amazon in South America which drains an area of almost seven million square kilometres. The Nile is the longest river. From its source in eastern Africa, it flows nearly 7000 kilometres northwards to the Mediterranean Sea.

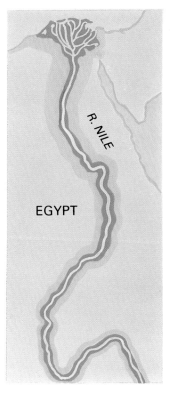

Egypt is a hot, dry country and the Nile is the main source of water. Most Egyptians live within 12 kilometres of the river.

The Ancient Egyptians invented the *shaduf*, a device for raising water from the river to pour over the land. They dug canals that carried the water out to dry land.

The Water Cycle

Rivers pour tonnes and tonnes of water into the oceans every day. Where does the water go to? Where does it come from? The answer is that water is continually on the move, constantly being exchanged between the land and the sea. This endless circulation is called the *water cycle*.

The Ocean Reservoir

More than 97 per cent of all the water on Earth is in the oceans. Most of the rest is in the polar ice caps and glaciers. Less than one per cent is circulating in the water cycle at any one time.

The cycle is powered by the Sun. The Sun's heat evaporates water on the surface of the ocean. This water is turned into invisible water vapour, which is a gas. It 'disappears into thin air' and is swept away by winds.

Up in the Air, Down to Earth

High ground on land forces the winds to rise. As the air rises, it cools and can no longer hold all of the water vapour in it. The vapour condenses – it liquefies into tiny droplets of water (or ice crystals if it is very cold). Masses of these droplets form clouds. The droplets merge together to form bigger droplets. These are raindrops which fall to land when it rains. (Ice crystals form snowflakes and fall as snow.)

Rain (or snow) occurs wherever warm, water-laden air is forced to rise, not solely over the mountains. Nearly three-quarters of the water vapour evaporated from the oceans falls back into them as rain. The rest

The water cycle is a continuous circulation of water, evaporating from the oceans, being carried to the land and dumped, and then flowing in rivers, and in rocks underground, back to the sea.

falls on land. Some runs straight into rivers, but most of it falls on to soil which soaks it up like a sponge. The water seeps through the soil and into the rock below. This water will eventually find its way back into a river, though it may be a long time after it has stopped raining. This is why rivers continue to flow for days or even months after the last rain. Once the water has joined a river, it begins its travels back to the sea where its journey began.

YOUNG RIVER
Water trickles from its source – here a melting glacier. The clear water rushes along, seeming always to be in a hurry. It pushes loose stones and pebbles down the slopes, and tumbles over waterfalls and rapids. The force of the water carves a steep-sided valley out of the rocks.

MATURE RIVER
As the river swings into maturity, its water becomes less clear. It is coloured by bits of rock, sand and clay picked up on its course. More and more water from tributaries and from rain flows into it.

OLD AGE
Burdened with its increased volume of water and sediment, the old river widens. The river channel is almost level, so the water moves slowly as it travels across its flood plain. It winds in great loops, sometimes abandoning its former course and leaving small lakes stranded. Finally it reaches the sea and dumps its load of water and sediment.

A River's Life Story

Most rivers are born in the mountains and flow relentlessly down to the sea. Small or great, they follow much the same course. The stages in their life can be divided into three parts: youth, maturity and old age.

A river and its tributaries often make a pattern like a tree's roots. The whole region drained by a river and its tributaries is called a river basin. Hills often border a river basin.

Fast and Furious

In the mountains, the river is young. It is narrow and flows swiftly over the rocks. The running water carries pieces of rock that cut into the ground below and gouge out holes. These merge together and lower the river bed. The valley grows deeper and its sides are steep.

Slowing Down

Beyond the mountains, the valley widens and its sides are less steep. The river becomes wider and deeper as more and more tributaries flow into it. Now in its mature stage, it flows more slowly, but still vigorously, swinging from side to side across the valley floor in a series of curves called *meanders*.

High ground may separate one river basin from another. Rain falling on the high ground drains into one or other of the two basins. The boundary which separates the two basins is called a *watershed* or divide.

Old Age

As the land becomes flatter, the river slows down. It is now in its old age and nearing the end of its journey. Heavy with the water it has gathered, it winds across a flat plain. The plain is covered by grains of sand, rock and clay that the river has brought down over the centuries from the upper part of its course. What it does not dump on the land during floods the river carries with it to the sea. Sometimes the sediments form new land areas called *deltas*.

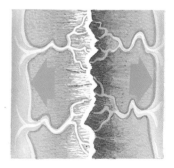

Springs occur where tilted, water-bearing rocks meet the surface. Rain falling on the hillside seeps into the rock, travels through it, and gushes or trickles out of the ground.

How Rivers Begin

Rainwater sinks into the soil and continues sinking until it meets rock. If the rock is *permeable,* the water continues to sink. Permeable rock allows water to pass through it. Rainwater flows through permeable rocks until it reaches a barrier of *impermeable,* or compact, rock. Water cannot flow through impermeable rock, so its passage is blocked. The water flows along the top of the impermeable rock until it seeps to the surface. There it may bubble out in one place as a spring, or lie at the surface as a wet bog. Many springs or bogs supply enough water to form a lake. Spring water is often clean and fresh because the fine pores of the rock filter the water.

Bogs and lakes may also occur in hollows on hillsides, as a result of rainwater collecting in them. The soil there becomes saturated and the water seeps out to become the source of a stream. Rivers also start at the ends of glaciers where the ice melts.

Permeable rocks can be either porous or non-porous. A porous rock like sandstone (below) is hard but it contains tiny pores through which water can seep. Limestone (above) is non-porous. The rock is solid, but it has many cracks in it.

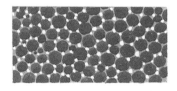

Rivers Underground

When rain falls on hills and mountains, it mostly runs away in streams and rivers. But if the rock the land is made of is limestone, the rain sinks into it. Limestone is full of tiny cracks, through which the water seeps. Rainwater is not pure water. It has carbon dioxide from the air dissolved in it, which makes it slightly acidic. The acid is very weak, but little by little it can dissolve limestone. Over thousands of years, the acid rain eats away tunnels in the rock. Water collects in these tunnels and they become rivers underground, which run into huge caverns in the limestone.

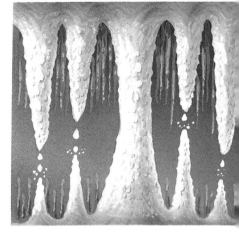

Water finds the gaps in limestone rock and enlarges them to form shafts and tunnels. Sometimes a stream on land disappears down a shaft and becomes an underground waterfall. The water continues to wear away the limestone and form a maze of underground passageways and caverns. Water droplets that fall to the cave floor leave deposits of rock particles. These build up into stalagmites. The drops leave similar deposits on the roof and they grow into stalactites. Sometimes the two meet and form a solid column.

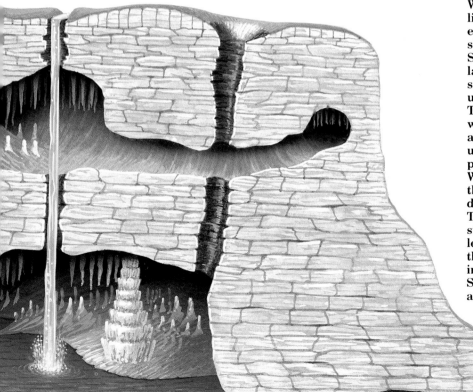

Rivers Shape the Land

In rainy places, rain and rivers work together to erode, or shape, the land. In its young stage, the river bed is worn away by stones which the swift-flowing current pushes downhill. The stones constantly scrape and scour the river bed, until a steep-sided, V-shaped valley is etched into the hillside.

All the time, raindrops batter the valley sides, like billions of sharp chisels. They loosen splinters of rock and splash fine grains of soil into the air. The rainwater floods downhill, washing these particles along with it, into the river at the bottom of the valley. The river sweeps them away, its violent motion breaking them down into smaller and smaller pieces, called sediment.

A river sorts its load into light things at the top, and heavy at the bottom. Tiny clay particles are light, so they float near the surface. Sand grains bob up and down nearer the bottom. Heavy rocks are rolled along the bed. The lightest material moves along the middle of the channel where the current is swiftest, the heaviest is at the bottom and sides. Half the river's load cannot be seen, because it is dissolved in the water.

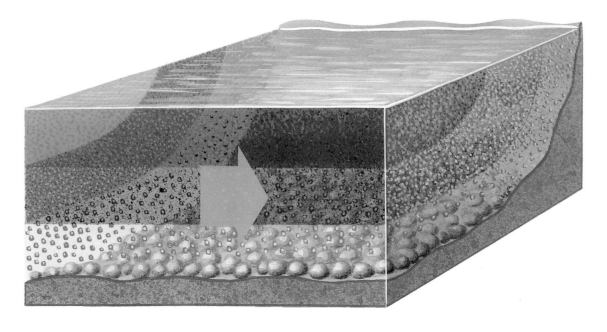

Waterfalls

When the river is young it is in a hurry. The water flows swiftly down steeply sloping channels, gouging out the river bed as it goes. If you stand by a mountain stream you can even hear the grinding noise as the stones dragged over the river bed grind and wear away the rock. Some rocks, such as granite, are hard to wear away. Soft rocks, such as clay, are easier. When the river flows over a place where hard rock gives way to soft, the soft rock is worn away more rapidly. Here rapids and waterfalls occur, where the edge of the hard rock is left like a step over which the river plunges.

As the water with its load of rocks hits the bottom, more of the soft rock is worn away and the falls get taller. The falling water and stones often wear out a basin, called a plunge pool, at the bottom of the falls.

Falling water undercuts the softer rocks at the base of the falls, leaving the hard rock above sticking out – like a shelf without a support. Now and then, pieces of the shelf break off, and the edge of the falls is moved farther back upstream. Niagara Falls in North America are retreating like this, by an average of a metre every year. Eventually they will disappear.

The Mature River

After the river has left the hills and mountains it begins its mature stage. It flows over a more gently sloping bed, but it still runs fast because there are fewer rocks or sharp bends to slow it down. Water seeps into it along its banks, and other rivers join it so it gets bigger all the time. After heavy rain, the river water becomes less clear. It is coloured by mud and sediment washed into it from the sides of its valley.

The current on the outside edge of each bend is faster than on the inside. On the outside, the river wears away its bank, so that it is almost like a cliff. On the inside, where the current is slower, the river dumps some of the sediment it is carrying. This builds up by the edge and the bank grows out into the river.

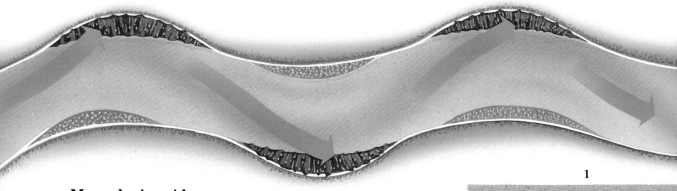

1

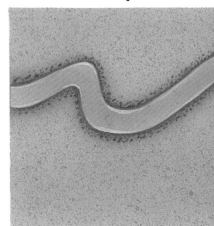

Meandering Along

In its mature stage a river flows in a series of S-bends, called meanders. When the river flows round a bend, the water and its load of mud and sediment swing towards the outside bank. Here the river is at its deepest. All the time, the river is wearing this bank away, but on the inner bank on the other side of the river the opposite is happening. The water slows and drops part of its load as *silt* at the foot of this bank. This goes on and on; slowly, the silt piles up. It becomes part of the gently sloping bank, which creeps farther and farther out into the river.

You can see what happens to the bed of the meandering river. On the outside of each bend, the sides are steep; on the inside, the sediment piles up in a more gentle slope.

As the river meanders (1), it erodes the outside bank and builds up the inside one. This changes the shape of the meander, from a wide curve to a narrow loop (2). When it floods, the river rises over its banks and takes a short cut across the two ends of the loop. In time it wears out a new channel (3), and this direct route becomes the main channel. The old course of the river is abandoned. Its remains become an ox-bow lake.

An Ox-bow Lake

All the time, the river is changing the shape of the meander. One bank is being worn away; the other is being added to. Gradually, the wide meander bend becomes a narrow loop.

One day, perhaps during a flood, the river cuts across the neck of the loop. Quickly it wears out a channel and becomes straight. Eventually the loop is cut off from the river and becomes an *ox-bow* lake.

2

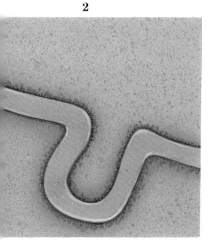

3

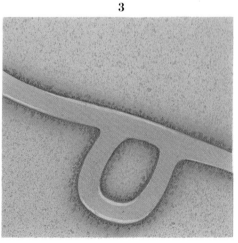

4

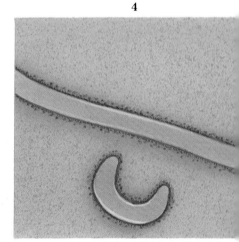

15

Old Age

In old age, the river flows slowly across a nearly level plain, called its *flood plain*. The plain is covered with layer upon layer of sediment which the river has brought down from higher up its course and deposited on the land during periodic floods.

Floods may be caused by heavy rain or melting snow in the mountains, which swell the volume of the river and make it flow faster. In times of flood, gigantic quantities of soil and rock may be torn from the banks and transported downstream. On the flood plain, the swollen river may overflow its banks and fan out over the low-lying land on either side. It dumps the larger, heavier particles of rock along its banks, and spreads the finer sediments across the land.

The flood plain of the river. In old age the river's work of erosion is over. Now it is adding to the land. Deposits of silt and sediment build up by the river banks. These embankments are called levees. At the same time the river bed builds up as more and more sediment comes to rest on it. As a result, the river bed is often raised above the level of the surrounding land. This means that floods are frequent and levees often have to be reinforced to prevent them.

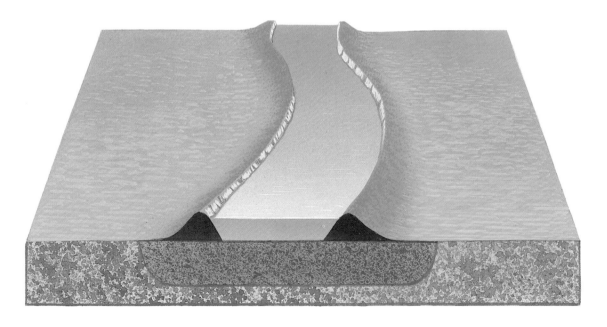

Journey's End

Most rivers carry huge loads of sediment into the sea. As the river flows into the sea, the current slackens and drops sand and mud on the sea floor. Unless high tides or strong currents wash it away, the sediment grows to form new land, called a *delta*. The new land extends out to sea in a roughly triangular shape.

Deltas make good farmland. The soil is deep and fertile, and there are hardly any large rocks or stones in it, so it is easy to work. Even if there is little rainfall, the river is close enough to provide fresh water for growing crops.

Although deltas attract people because of their rich soil, they are often dangerous places to live. Most are flat and scarcely above sea level. They are easily flooded by their river or by high tides.

1

2

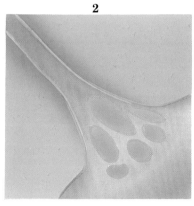

3

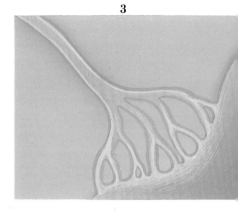

A river drops its load of sediment as it enters the sea. In some places, high tides or swift ocean currents sweep the sediment away. The river mouth remains open, like a funnel, and is called an estuary (1).

In other places, the sediment is not carried away. It builds up into sand and mud banks in the mouth of the river (2). More sediment collects and blocks the river mouth completely, forming an

extension of the land. The river splits up into a maze of smaller streams that flow across the top of the new land to the sea (3). This kind of river mouth is called a delta.

Rivers Made Young

Over millions of years, rivers can wear down even the highest mountains to almost flat plains. The rivers then flow slowly over this gentle land, meandering to the sea. But land does not always stay the same. Sometimes quite spectacular changes take place that make an old river young again.

Movements in the Earth's crust may squeeze rocks, and crumple the land up into new mountain ranges. Sometimes huge blocks of land are pushed upwards. Sometimes the sea level drops. When these things happen a lazy old river may be jolted out of its lethargy. Instead of crossing flat land, it must flow once again down steep slopes, like a juvenile river, racing towards the sea. This process is called *rejuvenation*.

Carving a New Passage

As it runs faster, the river's energy increases. It uses its new energy to erode its bed. The swift stream cuts a new, much deeper valley in the floor of the old one. But it does not remove all the original floor. Parts of it are left, like shelves, high and dry above the bottom of the new valley. They are called *river terraces*. Many cities have been built on river terraces because they are flat, there is water nearby, and only the highest floods can reach them.

The most spectacular example of the power of a rejuvenated river is the Grand Canyon in the United States. Ten million years ago, the Colorado River meandered lazily over its broad flood plain, just above sea level. The same earth movements which created the Rocky Mountains gradually raised the flood plain

In old age, the river has a wide flood plain barely above sea level (1). If the land rises, or the sea level falls, the river cuts a new channel down into the old flood plain (2). Parts of the original flood plain are left behind as terraces, facing each other across the new river valley (3).

by 2500 metres. As the land rose, the Colorado ran faster because it had farther to fall before it reached the sea. The river then started to carve out its magnificent canyon. So far, it is 350 kilometres long, up to 20 kilometres wide, and nearly two kilometres deep in places. It winds to and fro along the same twisting course as it did ten million years ago, over its flood plain. Still at work, the Colorado is gouging its channel deeper and deeper at the rate of one centimetre every 70 years.

Two million million cubic metres of rock have been washed away by the Colorado River to make the Grand Canyon. Canyons are created in dry areas. Nearly all the erosion is done by the river; there is not enough rain to help wear away the valley sides, so they remain like sheer cliffs rising up from the river.

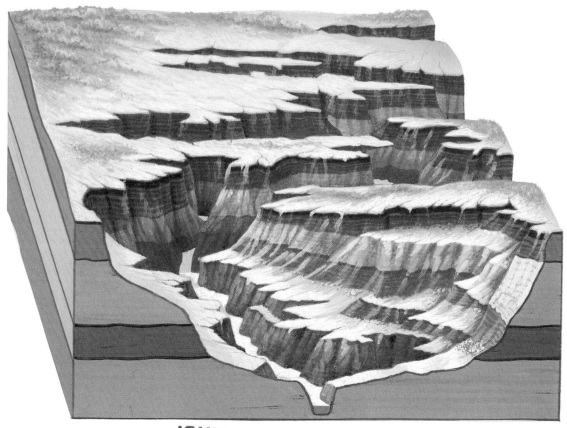

Floods

Floods occur when more water flows down a river than its banks can hold. Rain for weeks on end can cause floods, and so can particularly heavy storms. Some rivers that rise in high mountains flood every spring. The snow melts too quickly, and more water flows into the rivers than they can carry away.

Sometimes the floodwater breaks through the river banks. After the flood, the river may continue to flow

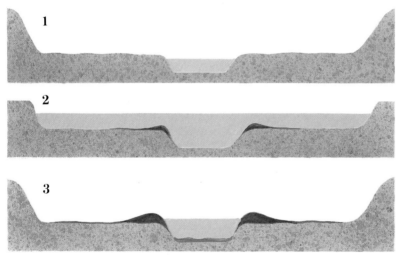

along the new channel it has made and never return to its old course. Sometimes the river overflows long stretches of its banks, covering the low-lying flood plain nearby with mud and fine silt.

Heavier material is dumped by the banks. In time this builds up into mounds called *levees*. People often strengthen levees artificially to prevent the river flooding.

Trees help to prevent floods (opposite). On a bare hillside, the rainwater rushes over the surface, carrying loose soil and rock with it.

The land beside the river is fertile because the river floods. As it nears the sea, the river is wide and shallow (1). It is full of mineral-rich sediments, washed into it in its upper reaches. When it floods, the sediments are deposited on the land, adding a fertile layer for crops to grow on (2). Gradually levees build up on the banks, which give some protection against future floods (3).

Dams (opposite) are often built to prevent floods. They hold back flood water by creating a lake behind the dam in which the water is stored. The water can then be released slowly so that the river does not overflow its banks downstream. The stored water can be used to create hydroelectric power and to irrigate farmland.

Floods may also be caused when forests are cut down on mountain slopes. Trees help to prevent floods. Their roots bind the soil, soak up water and keep the soil from being washed away. Their foliage acts as an umbrella, which breaks the force of the raindrops. The removal of trees increases the volume of water in the rivers, chokes them with mud, and causes floods downstream. The 1988 floods in Bangladesh were one result of the destruction of millions of trees along the Ganges and Brahmaputra rivers.

TENNESSEE TREES
In the 1920s, the basin of the Tennessee River was one of the poorest parts of the United States. Upstream, trees had been cut down, and in the valleys ploughed land was left unprotected in winter. Rain washed millions of tonnes of best topsoil into the streams, clogging them with silt. Downstream the muddy rivers flooded, turning good farmland into useless swamps. A scheme was introduced in the 1930s to control the floods with a chain of dams. This reduced the risk of flooding, and new trees and crops were planted to cut down the loss of soil. Today the area is thriving.

21

Life in a River

The speed of the current determines what animals and plants live where in a river; creatures can survive in fast currents only if they are powerful swimmers or if they can cling to the bottom. Plants cannot root until the current is slower and a certain amount of sediment has built up.

Stonefly

Dipper

Trout

Kingfisher

Purple loosestrife

Dragonfly

Moorhen

Heron

YOUNG RIVER
Trout live in scattered pools. There are insects in the water and birds like the dipper come to feed on them.

The beaver gnaws down trees to dam rivers. The family build a warm, safe home called a lodge behind the dam. The entrances to it are below the water, so no predators can reach them.

MATURE RIVER
Numerous fish, plants and insects. Kingfishers and herons feed on the fish. Dragonflies snap up insects in the air, and moorhens nest on the banks.

The otter builds a nest in the river bank and finds plenty of perch and carp to eat. There are numerous frogs and toads, small fishes and insects. In hot places, bigger animals like crocodiles and alligators bathe in the shallow waters.

In the headstream, where the water races over the rocks, the stream is narrow and shallow. Moss grows on the exposed rocks, and insects, such as mayflies and stoneflies, cling to them. A few snails and leeches hold fast to the rocks under the water.

As the water gathers strength, even the mosses disappear as the cold, fast-moving water carries the loose rocks along and scours the bottom with them. Here and there, there are deeper pools where you may find trout, one of the few fish strong enough to swim against the current.

Lower down the river broadens. Plants grow along the edges and in the smooth flowing water. There are plenty of fish in the water for the kingfisher to eat, and lots of insects for the water birds.

The water is even calmer as the river crosses its flood plain. There are eels, carp and pike in the water, and plenty of plants for the birds to nest in at the water's edge. The water becomes muddier and muddier as the river approaches the sea. Fewer creatures live here, where fresh water meets salt water, and the water level rises and falls with the tide.

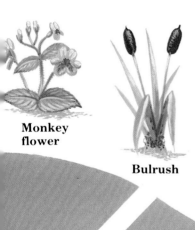

Monkey flower

Bulrush

Perch

Pike

Alligator

Otter

Terrapin

Rivers at Work and Play

People use rivers in many ways. Rivers everywhere provide water for drinking, for washing and for cleaning. In dry parts of the world people rely on rivers for water to grow food. Large areas which were once desert can now grow crops, or grass for sheep and cattle, by using water taken from rivers. Some of the best farmland in Australia and the United States was once desert. It has been made fertile by the use of river water.

River Power

Rivers can be made to turn wheels and drive machinery. For hundreds of years, water-wheels turned millstones, to grind flour for bread. Later, they were used to work machinery for making cloth. Today, we use rivers to make electricity. Water is stored behind a dam and led through pipes to turn a huge wheel called a turbine. The turbine drives a generator which produces electricity – hydroelectricity.

Nuclear power stations need water to cool their reactors, so they are built near rivers or by the sea. Factories need water to make goods and to carry away waste materials. All over the world factories are set up close to rivers. Boats can carry industrial products and heavy goods that take up a lot of space. Coal, iron-ore and steel are all transported by river more cheaply than by road or rail. In China 25 per cent of all goods go by river. The Chang Jiang is the country's most important highway.

Rivers are also used for sport and leisure. Swimming is the oldest water sport. The most popular is fishing.

The water and fertile soil of river valleys attracted ancient peoples. Instead of hunting for food or gathering berries, they settled by rivers, growing crops and domesticating animals.

In developed countries an average person uses over 300 litres of clean water a day. Only five are used for drinking and cooking. Most of the rest is needed for cleaning and sanitation – and watering our gardens.

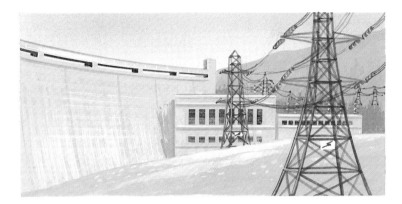

Water-wheels were once used to produce power for milling flour. Later, power from rivers was harnessed to work all kinds of machinery, from spinning machines to hammers.

A hydroelectric power station uses falling water to produce electrical energy. It is renewable energy, because the water is constantly replaced by rain and snow, and it is a clean form of power. It does not pollute the atmosphere, but the flooding of land behind the dam may cause problems. People lose their homes, the lake may be polluted and the balance of nature be upset.

River barges may be slow, but they carry heavy goods, such as coal and steel, more cheaply than trucks and trains. The River Rhine is the busiest river in the world, carrying shipping from the North Sea to Switzerland.

Rivers not only support life, they also make it more enjoyable. Fishing is one of the world's most popular pastimes. Millions of people use rivers for swimming, rowing, sailing and just messing about in boats.

Save our Streams

Rivers are vitally important to us. We use them all the time, but in so doing we also abuse them. The life in a river and the life on land that depends on the river exist in a delicate balance. If rivers are used carefully and looked after properly they will go on being useful. But if we treat them badly they can become a danger.

In the last 200 years, many rivers have been used as drains to carry away untreated sewage, and factory and farm wastes. As a result, the water has been poisoned, killing river creatures and harming anyone who drinks it. The Cuyahoga River, which flows into Lake Erie in the United States, became so polluted with oil and other chemicals that it caught fire!

1 DAMS
The damming of rivers brings great benefits but also drawbacks. Initially, farmland is drowned and people lose their homes. The dam traps fertile silt and deprives farmlands and fisheries of nutrients. In the stagnant waters of the lake, diseases may breed.

2 TOWNS
Towns and cities not only take water from rivers but return it to them – used. Human and vegetable waste decays quickly and, suitably treated, can be disposed of in rivers, so long as the population is not too great.

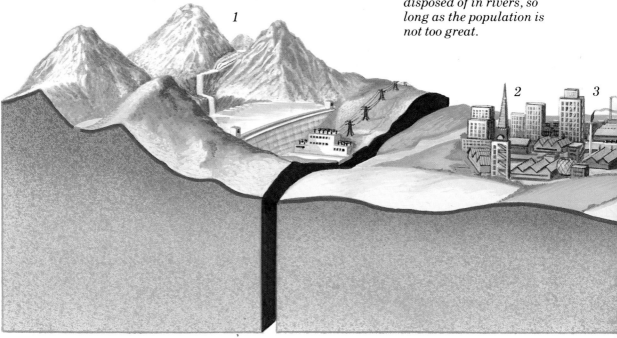

3 INDUSTRY
Poisonous chemicals are widely used in modern factories, and cleansing the waste is expensive. In most countries it is illegal to dump them, but sometimes the law has been disregarded – with disastrous consequences.

4 IRRIGATION
More and more water is taken from rivers to make crops grow. The Colorado is a mighty river as it flows through the Grand Canyon, but by the time it reaches the Pacific Ocean, it has lost so much water that it has become a trickle only a few metres wide.

The River Ganges in India remained remarkably clean for centuries. Today, more than 200 million people live in its basin, and the river cannot cope with the great mass of waste it receives daily. It has become a health hazard to all who use it.

Pollution controls, including special equipment to monitor and prevent industrial effluent, can help to save rivers. A costly and lengthy programme to cleanse the Cuyahoga and the whole Great Lakes area has been largely successful, as has a programme to clean up the Thames. So long as the river can flow steadily to keep its channel clean – which means no one must take too much water from it or put harmful substances into it – it can maintain its own healthy balance.

5 AGRICULTURE
Fertilizers washed into rivers cause water plants to flourish, sometimes so much that they clog up the river completely. Pesticides not only kill pests on the land, but fish and other wildlife in rivers.

6 SHIPPING
Barges, oil tankers and other vessels empty their bilge tanks and spill oil into rivers, killing fish and birds and plants. Water sports and pleasure boats frighten wildlife, ruining nests and feeding places.

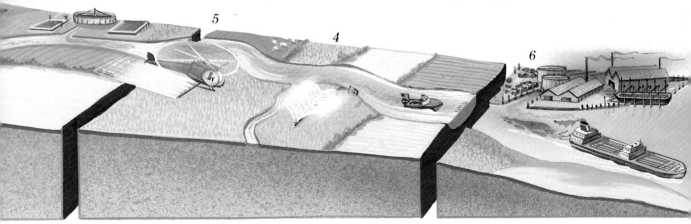

River
Profiles

NORTH AMERICA

Arkansas Rises in the Rocky Mountains in the United States and flows east to join Missouri River. Passes through Wichita, Tulsa and Little Rock. Length 2330 km.

Colorado Flows west from the Rocky Mountains in the United States to the Gulf of California. It has carved out the Grand Canyon in Arizona. Its vast Hoover Dam provides electricity for Los Angeles. Length 2330 km.

Columbia Rises in the Canadian Rockies, flows south into the United States and swings west to the Pacific. Its Grand Coulee Dam is the largest concrete structure in the world. Length 1950 km.

Mackenzie Flows north from Great Slave Lake in Canada to the Beaufort Sea in the Arctic Ocean. It is frozen from October to June. Length 1800 km.

Mississippi-Missouri Two rivers in the United States which are usually considered as a single system. The Mississippi rises near the Canadian border and flows south, to be joined at St Louis by the Missouri which rises in Montana. The Missouri is the longest river in the United States (3960 km). Together the rivers enter the Gulf of Mexico through an extensive delta. Their river basin is the third largest in the world. Length 6020 km.

Missouri See Mississippi-Missouri.

Nelson This is the old fur trappers' route from Lake Winnipeg in Canada to Hudson Bay. Length 740 km.

Ohio Rises in the Appalachian Mountains in the United States and runs west to join the Mississippi at Cairo, Illinois. Fully navigable, it is

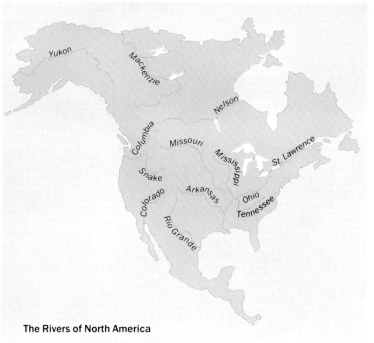

The Rivers of North America

important for freight. Pittsburgh and Cincinnati are on its banks. Length 1580 km.

Rio Grande Forms the border for 2000 km between United States and Mexico, where it is known as the Rio Bravo del Norte. Flows into the Gulf of Mexico. Length 2880 km.

St Lawrence Flows from Lake Ontario in Canada to the Atlantic Ocean. The St Lawrence Seaway, a system of canals, locks and dams, has opened the way for sea-going vessels from Montreal to the Great Lakes. Forms border between Canada and United States for 183 km. Length 1200 km.

Snake The major tributary of the Columbia River. Passes through its own Grand Canyon, which is 200 km long and up to 2408 m deep. Length 1610 km.

Tennessee Largest tributary of the Ohio, with a system of dams that control floods, provide hydroelectricity and make the river fully navigable. Length 1050 km.

Yukon Rises in Canadian Rockies and flows through Alaska to the Bering Sea. Icebound from October to June. Length 3190 km.

SOUTH AMERICA

Amazon Rises in the Andes Mountains in Peru, 150 km from the Pacific. Flows east across Brazil and into the Atlantic at the equator. The world's second longest river but easily the greatest; it contains a fifth of all the river water in the world. Its basin covers 7 million square km and is the world's largest area of tropical rain forest. Length 6450 km.

28

The Rivers of South America

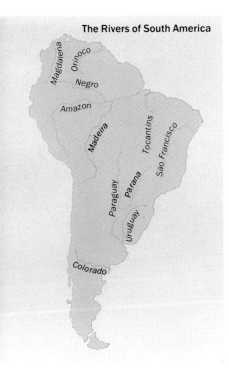

Colorado Rises in the Andes in Argentina. It flows east into the Atlantic through a delta south of Bahia Blanca. Length 1140 km.

Madeira Third longest river in South America. Rises in Andes Mountains in Bolivia and flows north-east through tropical rain forest to Brazil, to join the Amazon near Manaus. Length 3200 km.

Magdalena Rises in the Andes Mountains of Colombia and flows north into the Caribbean Sea through a wide delta. Length 1610 km.

Negro Rises in northern Brazil and is a tributary of the Amazon which it joins near Manaus. Its basin lies wholly in tropical rain forest. Its channel is more than 30 km wide in places. Length 2250 km.

Orinoco Chief river of Venezuela. It rises in the south and flows north along the Colombian border before turning east to the Atlantic. Length 2200 km.

Paraguay Branch of the Paraná that rises in Brazil and flows south through Asuncion, before joining Paraná. Length 1920 km.

Plata See Paraná; Uruguay.

Paraná Rises in eastern Brazil, runs south and forms part of the border between Brazil and Paraguay. It flows on through Argentina to the Rio de la Plata (River Plate) estuary and the South Atlantic. Its basin is the second largest in South America. Length 4000 km.

São Francisco Rises in the Minas Gerais Province of Brazil and is the main route to east Brazil. Has third largest basin in South America. Length 2900 km.

Tocantins Rises in central Brazil and flows north to Atlantic Ocean. Length 2500 km.

Uruguay Rises in southern Brazil and flows south to join the Rio de la Plata (River Plate). Forms part of border between Uruguay and Argentina, and between Argentina and Brazil. Length 1360 km.

ASIA

Amu Darya Rises in Pamir Mountains in central Asia and enters the Aral Sea through a large delta. Its ancient name was the River Oxus. Length 2400 km.

Amur Rises in northern Mongolia and flows into the Sea of Okhotsk. Forms border between Soviet Union and China for 1750 km. Its Chinese name is Heilong Jiang. Length 4350 km.

Brahmaputra Flows from the Chinese Himalayas through India and Bangladesh into the Bay of Bengal. Forms an enormous delta with the Ganges. Length 2900 km.

Chang Jiang (Yangtze Kiang) China's largest river and third longest in the world. It flows from mountains in south-western China through one of the most densely populated areas of the world and empties into the eastern China Sea at Shanghai. Its basin covers nearly 20 per cent of China. Length 6300 km.

Euphrates Flows from eastern Turkey through Syria into Iraq. Joined by Tigris to form Shatt al Arab waterway before emptying into The Gulf. Length 2730 km.

Ganges River sacred to Hindus. Rises in Indian Himalayas and flows through densely populated areas of northern India and Bangladesh. It enters the Bay of Bengal through a massive delta. Length 2510 km.

Huang He (Hwang Ho) flows from western China to Bo Hai Gulf. Its name which means Yellow River comes from the colour of its silty water. It is also called 'China's Sorrow' because of its frequent devastating floods. Length 4670 km.

Hwang Ho See Huang He.

Indus Rises in Tibet and flows south through Pakistan to northern Arabian Sea near Karachi. Length 2880 km.

Irrawaddy Flows north-south through the whole length of Burma to delta on the Andaman Sea. Length 2100 km.

Irtysh See Ob.

Kolyma Flows from the Kolyma Mountains of Siberia in the Soviet Union to the eastern Siberian Sea. Length 2600 km.

Lena Longest river entirely in the Soviet Union. Rises near Lake Baikal in southern Siberia and flows to a delta on the Laptev Sea. Length 4400 km.

Mekong Rises in Tibet and flows south through Laos, Thailand, Kampuchea and South Vietnam, and enters the South China Sea through an extensive, marshy delta. Length 4000 km.

Ob Rises in central Asia and, with its main tributary the River Irtysh, forms the Soviet Union's longest

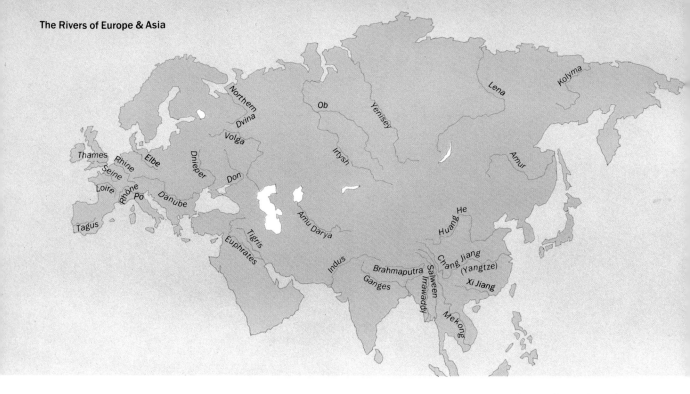

river system. Flows into the Arctic Ocean. Length (Ob-Irtysh) 5570 km.

Salween Rises in Tibet and flows through southern China and Burma into the Gulf of Martaban near Moulmein. Length 2810 km.

Shatt al Arab See Euphrates.

Si Kiang See Xi Jiang.

Tigris See Euphrates.

Xi Jiang (Si Kiang) Rises in southern China and flows east to the South China Sea south of Guangzhou (Canton). Length 2200 km.

Yangtze Kiang See Chang Jiang.

Yenisey Rises in central Siberia and flows north to the Arctic Ocean. Length 4100 km.

EUROPE

Danube Europe's second longest river, it flows from West Germany through Austria, Czechoslovakia, Hungary, Yugoslavia, Bulgaria and Romania to the Black Sea. Length 2850 km.

Dnieper Rises in the Valdai Hills near Smolensk in the Soviet Union and flows south to the Black Sea. Length 2200 km.

Don Rises south of Moscow in the Soviet Union and flows into the Sea of Azov. Length 1870 km.

Elbe Flows from its source in Czechoslovakia through East and West Germany to the North Sea. Length 1160 km.

Loire Longest river in France. It rises in the Massif Central and flows into the Bay of Biscay near Nantes. Length 1020 km.

Northern Dvina Highly commercial river in north-west of Soviet Union. Flows into White Sea near Archangel. Length 740 km.

Po Italy's longest river. It flows from the Alps to the Adriatic near Venice. Length 650 km.

Rhine The major waterway of western Europe. From its source in the Swiss Alps, it flows through Austria, becomes the border between France and West Germany, and splits into a delta in the Netherlands where it empties into the North Sea. Length 1320 km.

Rhone Flows from Swiss Alps into France and south to the Mediterranean Sea. Length 870 km.

Seine Rises in central France and flows north, passing through Rouen and Paris, to the English Channel. Length 780 km.

Tagus Rises in Spain and flows through Portugal to the Atlantic. Length 1010 km.

Thames From its source in the Cotswold Hills in England, flows by Oxford and through London to the North Sea. Length 340 km.

Volga The longest river in Europe. It rises in the Valdai Hills in the Soviet Union and flows through Volgograd to its estuary on the Caspian Sea near Astrakhan. Length 3690 km.

AFRICA

Congo See Zaire.

Limpopo Also called the Crocodile River. Rises in South Africa, and flows eastwards, forming part of the border with Zimbabwe, through Mozambique and into the Indian Ocean. Length 1600 km.

Niger Rises on the border between Sierra Leone and Guinea. It flows north, and then sweeps south through Nigeria to its delta in the Gulf of Guinea. It is the third longest river in Africa and has the biggest delta. Length 4100 km.

Nile The longest river in the world. It rises near the equator and flows north through the Egyptian desert to its huge delta on the Mediterranean Sea. Its two main branches are the White Nile which starts at Lake Victoria in Uganda and the Blue Nile whose source is Lake Tana. The Blue Nile joins the White at Khartoum in Sudan. From there it is simply called the Nile. At intervals there are cataracts (rapids) and several dams, including the Aswan Dam. Length 6670 km.

Orange Rises in Drakensberg Mountains in Lesotho. It flows into South Africa and forms border with Namibia. It enters the Atlantic at Alexander Bay. Length 2100 km.

Senegal Rises in Guinea in west Africa and flows north through Mali and then forms the border between Senegal and Mauritania all the way to the Atlantic. Length 1600 km.

Volta Rises in Burkina Faso and flows through Ghana into Gulf of Guinea at Ada. There are three arms: the Black, White and Red Volta rivers. The Akosombo Dam has created Lake Volta. Length 1500 km.

Zaire (Congo) Forms part of the boundary between the countries of Zaire and Congo for part of its course, and both names are used for it. Its chief headstream is the Lualaba. It drains the second largest river basin in the world. Length 4670 km.

Zambezi Rises in northern Zambia and forms the border between Zambia and Zimbabwe. It flows into the Indian Ocean through a delta in Mozambique. Runs over the Victoria Falls. Length 2700 km.

AUSTRALIA AND NEW ZEALAND

Darling Tributary of River Murray in New South Wales and part of major irrigation and hydroelectric power schemes. Longer than the Murray but intermittent. Length 2740 km.

Murray Australia's longest permanently flowing river. Rises in the Snowy Mountains in the Australian Alps and flows west into Encounter Bay. For 2000 km it forms the border between Victoria and New South Wales. Part of major irrigation and hydroelectricity system. Length 2570 km.

Waikato New Zealand's longest river. Flows north-west from the centre of North Island to the Tasman Sea south of Auckland. Length 425 km.

Wanganui Rises in centre of North Island and flows south into Tasman Sea. Famed for its beauty. Length 425 km.

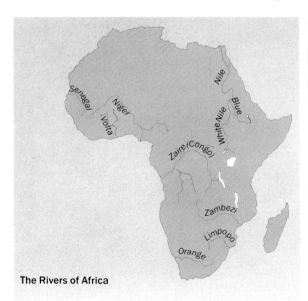

The Rivers of Africa

The Rivers of Australia & New Zealand

Index